Living in
POLAR REGIONS

Tea Benduhn

Reading consultant: Susan Nations, M.Ed., author/literacy coach/
consultant in literacy development

WEEKLY READER®
PUBLISHING

Please visit our web site at: www.garethstevens.com
For a free color catalog describing our list of high-quality books,
call 1-800-542-2595 (USA) or 1-800-387-3178 (Canada).

Library of Congress Cataloging-in-Publication Data

Benduhn, Tea.
      Living in polar regions / Tea Benduhn.
        p. cm. — (Life on the edge)
      ISBN-10: 0-8368-8343-8 (lib. bdg.)
      ISBN-13: 978-0-8368-8343-5 (lib. bdg.)
      ISBN-10: 0-8368-8348-9 (softcover)
      ISBN-13: 978-0-8368-8348-0 (softcover)
      1. Polar regions—Juvenile literature.   2. Polar regions—
Social life and customs—Juvenile literature.   I. Title.
      G587.B46   2008
      910.911—dc22   2007014705

This edition first published in 2008 by
Weekly Reader® Books
An imprint of Gareth Stevens Publishing
1 Reader's Digest Road
Pleasantville, NY 10570-7000 USA

Copyright © 2008 by Gareth Stevens, Inc.

Managing editor: Mark Sachner
Art direction: Tammy West
Picture research: Sabrina Crewe
Production: Jessica Yanke

Picture credits: cover, title page Dean Conger/National Geographic/Getty Images; p. 5 © Galen Rowell/
Corbis; pp. 6, 7 Scott Krall/© Gareth Stevens, Inc.; p. 9 Theo Allofs/Riser/Getty Images; p. 10 Tatyana
Makeyeva/AFP/Getty Images; p. 11 © Graham Neden/Ecoscene/Corbis; p. 13 Bill Curtsinger/National
Geographic/Getty Images; p. 14 © Hans Reinhard/ Zefa/Corbis; p. 15 Ralph Crane/Time & Life Pictures/
Getty Images; p. 16 © Layne Kennedy/Corbis; p. 17 Richard Olsenius/National Geographic/Getty Images;
p. 19 © Gary Braasch/Corbis; p. 20 NASA; p. 21 AFP/Getty Images.

Printed in the United States of America

1 2 3 4 5 6 7 8 9 11 10 09 08 07

TABLE OF CONTENTS

Cover and title page: People use reindeer to pull sleds in the Arctic.

CHAPTER *1*

Welcome to the Polar Regions

The temperature is far below freezing. Ice, snow, and sky are all you can see for miles. There are no buildings or trees. There are no people. You are colder than you have ever been in your life. You might freeze to death if you do not find shelter. Where are you? You are in a polar region!

Earth has two polar regions. They are the areas around the North Pole and the South Pole. No other places on Earth are as cold as these areas. Very few plants can grow there. Very few animals live there. Almost no people live in the polar regions. Polar regions are **extreme** places to live.

Antarctica is a polar region. It can be a lonely place.

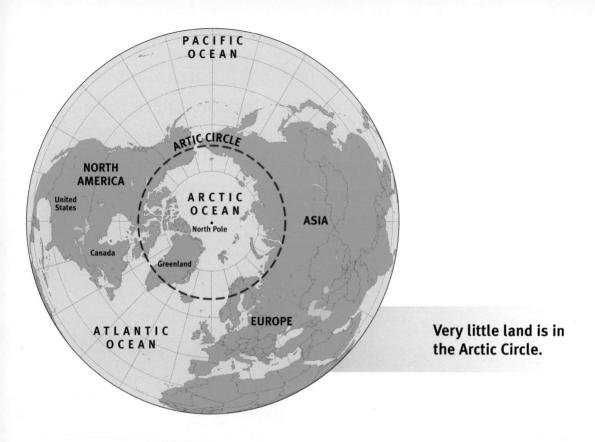

Very little land is in the Arctic Circle.

The area around the North Pole is called the Arctic Circle. Most of it is a frozen ocean. The only land in the Arctic Circle is around the edges. The land includes the northern parts of Europe, Asia, and North America. Most of Greenland is in the Arctic Circle.

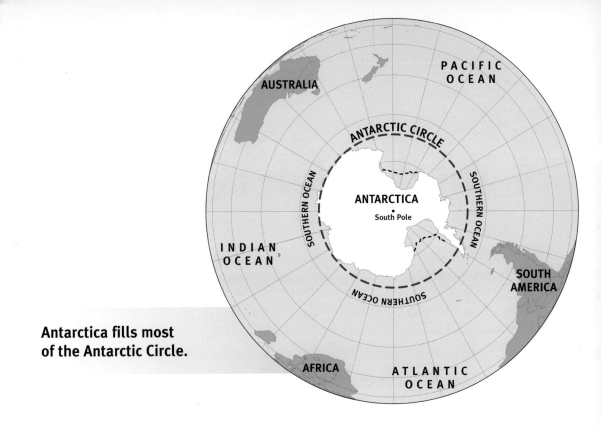

PACIFIC OCEAN

AUSTRALIA

ANTARCTIC CIRCLE

SOUTHERN OCEAN

SOUTHERN OCEAN

ANTARCTICA
· South Pole

INDIAN OCEAN

SOUTH AMERICA

SOUTHERN OCEAN

AFRICA

ATLANTIC OCEAN

Antarctica fills most of the Antarctic Circle.

The South Pole is located on the continent of Antarctica. Land fills most of the Antarctic Circle. No one lives in Antarctica year round, and it does not belong to any country. Many of the world's nations work together to **protect** the **environment** in Antarctica.

CHAPTER 2

People of the Polar Regions

The lowest temperature ever recorded on Earth was recorded in a polar region. It was −129° Fahrenheit (−89° Celsius)! People living and working in the polar regions are not afraid of the extreme weather and climate. Many people hunt birds, fish, and other animals. These people have everything they need to survive. Some of them make their homes in the polar regions.

For hundreds of years, **Native** people have lived in the Arctic Circle. Each group of people has its own way of life. The groups hunt different animals. They build different types of shelter, too. In North America, for example, many Inuit people build homes in dome shapes.

Today, many Inuit people still build dome-shaped homes to use during hunting and fishing trips. The entrance is an underground tunnel that keeps out cold air.

These Nenet people depend on reindeer for food, shelter, and getting around their homeland in northern Russia.

People living in the Arctic Circle **depend** on the animals they hunt. The Nenet people, for example, live in northern Russia. They follow reindeer, which move north in summer and south in winter. Some Nenet people still build homes out of poles and reindeer skins. They take down their homes and move them on sleds that reindeer pull.

Until **recently**, no one has lived in Antarctica. Today, scientists from all over the world stay there for parts of the year. They build research stations to live in. They study Antarctica's weather, land, and wildlife.

Scientists use machines that can work in the extreme cold.

CHAPTER 3

Living in the Polar Regions

The ground is frozen most of the year in the polar regions. Very few plants are able to grow, and people do not farm. The only plants that do grow are small, such as moss. Animals, however, can eat these small plants. People hunt these animals to get the **nutrients** they need to live.

Long ago, whales were important to the Inuit way of life.

Inuit people hunt many kinds of animals, including moose and caribou. Along the coast, they catch lots of fish. Long ago, Inuits hunted whales and seals, too. They used these animals' **blubber** to make oil, which they burned for heat. They had special rules for hunting these animals. They believed they could only hunt these animals if they treated them with **respect**.

The Sami people live in Norway, Sweden, Finland, and Russia. They are reindeer **herders**. Like Nenet people, they use every part of the reindeer. They can drink reindeer milk and eat reindeer meat. They use reindeer skins to make warm clothes.

The Sami people make and wear brightly-colored clothes.

14

Family is important to Inuits and other Arctic people. People learn what they need to know from their **elders**. Elders teach young people about the weather. They teach them how to hunt. They also teach important lessons about life.

Inuit elders teach children how to catch fish.

Huskies are great at pulling sleds! They have thick fur coats, which keep them warm.

The polar regions are mostly covered with ice and snow. It can be hard to get around. To walk, some people wear snowshoes, which look like huge tennis rackets. In the Arctic, people have traveled by sled for hundreds of years. They have used huskies, reindeer, or caribou to pull their sleds.

Today, most people use modern machines to travel in the polar regions. Scientists arrive in huge ships. People fly in **helicopters**. Instead of sleds, people use snowmobiles. These machines move fast, but they use gas and oil, and they **pollute** the air.

Snowmobiles can hurt the ground beneath the snow and ice, making it harder for plants to grow in summer.

CHAPTER *4*

People and the Polar Regions Today

The polar regions have many **resources**. Companies drill for oil in Alaska and pump natural gas in northern Russia. They mine **minerals** in many areas of the Arctic Circle. Wildlife that lives in these areas is in danger of dying out. These activities harm the way many people live and work in the Arctic.

Mining and drilling for oil and gas cause **pollution**. Companies build pipes that stretch for hundreds of miles. They pump oil through these pipes to huge **supertankers**. Sometimes, these pipes leak or the supertankers spill. Spilled oil harms the land and can kill animals.

When oil is spilled, people must work to clean it up. Volunteers try to save wildlife by cleaning off the oil.

These pictures were taken from outer space. They show how much of the ice around the North Pole has melted between the summer of 1979 (left) and the summer of 2003 (right).

Using oil and gas can lead to **global warming**. Global warming causes ice to melt in the polar regions. The melted ice can make the oceans warmer. If enough polar ice melts, sea levels could rise. Cities on coasts, such as New York, could be in danger of flooding.

Scientists want to protect the polar regions. Today, many scientists in Antarctica study the climate. They are trying to find ways to slow down global warming. Many nations are working to lower pollution. Protecting the polar regions may help save our planet.

These scientists are taking samples of Antarctic ice.

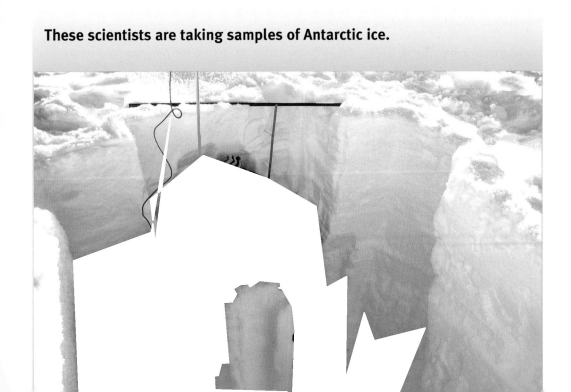

Glossary

blubber — a thick layer of fat under an animal's skin

climate – the weather and temperature usually found in an area

elders – people who are older than most others and have gained much knowledge with their age

environment – the natural things that make up a place

extreme – more of something, such as cold, than we are used to

global warming – the warming of Earth by gases that have been released into the atmosphere. These gases trap heat, and so Earth warms up.

herders – people who gather together groups of animals

minerals – substances other than plants that can be dug from the ground

Native – having to do with the types of people, animals, or plants that first lived in a certain place

nutrients – substances that help living things grow

pollute – to spoil the environment with human-made waste

pollution – human-made waste that harms the environment

resources – natural substances that people can use to improve their lives

respect – think of highly and treat kindly

supertankers – huge ships for carrying liquids

For More Information

Books

Antarctica. The Seven Continents (series). A. R. Schaefer
  (Bridgestone)

Arctic. DK 24 Hours (series). DK Publishing (DK Children)

Ituko — An Inuit Child. Children of the World (series).
  Francois Goalec (Blackbirch)

What Polar Animals Eat. Nature's Food Chains (series).
  Joanne Mattern (Gareth Stevens)

Web Sites

Tundra
www.mbgnet.net/sets/tundra/index.htm
Click on the links to find out more about the frozen world.

Wild Arctic Fun Guide
www.seaworld.org/fun-zone/fun-guides/arctic/index.htm
Get wild about the Arctic!

Index

About the Author

Tea Benduhn writes and edits books for children and teens. She lives in the beautiful state of Wisconsin with her husband and two cats. The walls of their home are lined with bookshelves filled with books. Tea says, "I read every day. It is more fun than watching television!"